PARK COUNTY PUBLIC LIBRARY
GUFFEY BRANCH

DATE DUE

Let's Eat
Dinner

Clare Hibbert

PARK COUNTY PUBLIC LIBRARY
GUFFEY BRANCH

Cherrytree books are distributed in the United States by
Black Rabbit BooksP.O. Box 3263, Mankato, MN, 56002

U.S. publication copyright © Cherrytree Books 2008
International copyright reserved in all countries.
No part of this book may be reproduced in any
form without written permission from the publisher.
Printed in China by WKT Company Ltd.

Library of Congress Cataloging-in-Publication Data
Hibbert, Clare, 1970-
   Let's eat dinner / Clare Hibbert. -- 1st ed.
       p. cm. -- (Sparkers)
   Originally published: London : Evans Brothers Ltd., 2007.
   Includes index.
   Summary: "Covers a range of healthy dinners from around the world
and where some foods come from. Includes simple recipe"--Provided by publisher.
   ISBN-13: 978-1-84234-529-0
   ISBN-10: 1-84234-529-X
   1. Dinners and dining--Juvenile literature. I. Title. II. Series.

TX737.H63 2009
641.5'4--dc22

                                                2007046383

First edition
9 8 7 6 5 4 3 2 1

First published in 2007 by Evans Brothers Ltd.
2A Portman Mansions, Chiltern Street, London W1U 6NR, United Kingdom

Produced for Evans Brothers Limited by
White-Thomson Publishing Ltd.

Copyright © Evans Brothers Limited 2007
Educational consultant: Sue Palmer MEd FRSA FEA
Project manager: Clare Hibbert
Picture research: Amy Sparks
Design: Balley Design Limited
Creative director: Simon Balley
Designer/Illustrator: Michelle Tilly

Contents

Dinnertime

This book is about **dinner**.

What time do **you** eat **your** dinner?

5

Getting Ready

How do you **help** make dinner?

tablecloth

Who sets the table in your house?

7

Rice

Rice is nice!

Do you eat rice with your dinner?

8

splosh

Rice grows in hot, rainy countries.

9

broccoli

cauliflower

pepper

How do you like them cooked?

11

Food from the Sea

Which fish do you
like to eat?

mussel

This is a tasty fish stew.

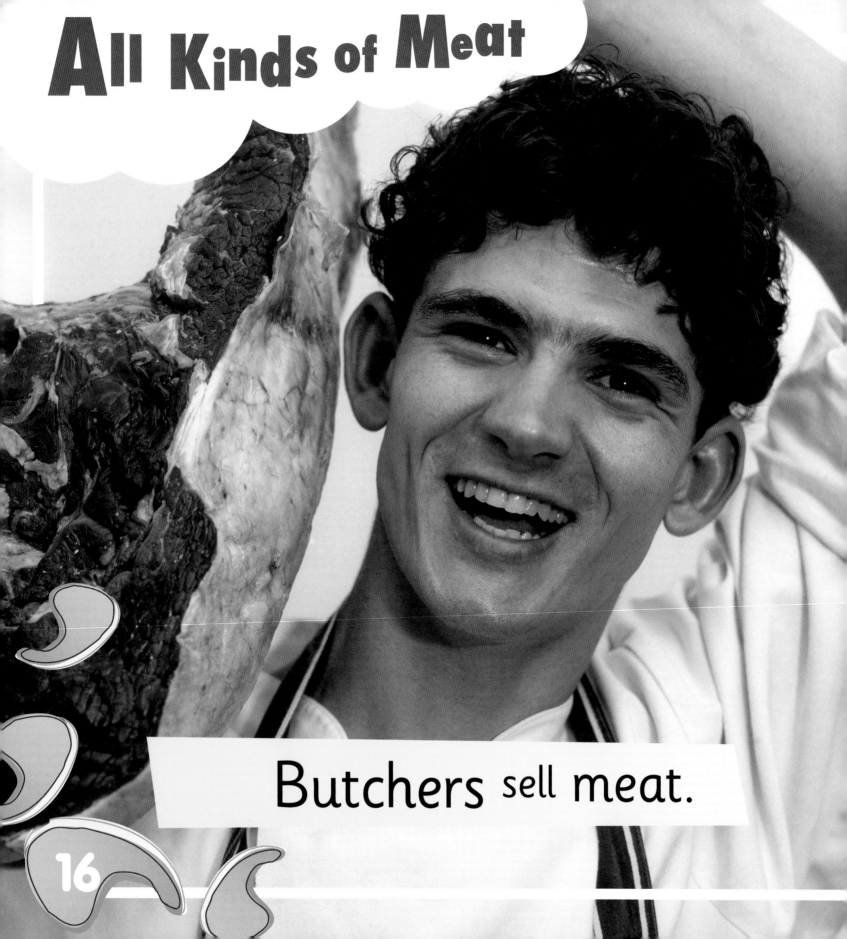

All Kinds of Meat

Butchers sell meat.

lamb kebab

What's your favorite meat dinner?

Desserts

Me first!

18

When do you like cold desserts?

apple pie

When do you like hot desserts?

19

Make It: Raita

Mix these things together to make raita.

- cucumber ✓
- plain yogurt ✓
- ground cumin ✓
- lemon juice ✓

naan

Raita tastes good with an Indian curry and naan bread.

Notes for Adults

Sparklers books are designed to support and extend the learning of young children. The books' high-interest subjects broaden young readers' knowledge and interests, making them ideal teaching tools as well.

Themed titles
Let's Eat Dinner is one of four *Food We Eat* titles that explore food and meals from around the world. The other titles are:
Let's Eat Breakfast   Let's Eat Lunch   Celebration Food

Areas of learning
Each *Food We Eat* title introduces educational concepts (such as personal development, literacy and mathematical skills) with subtlety and care. Children increase their knowledge and understanding of the world while developing their creativity.

Reading together
When sharing this book with younger children, take time to explore the pictures together. Encourage children by asking them to find, identify, count or describe different objects. Point out different colors or textures.

Allow quiet spaces in your reading so that children can ask questions or repeat your words. Try pausing mid-sentence so children can predict the next word. This sort of participation develops early reading skills.

Follow the words with your finger as you read them aloud. The main text is in Infant Sassoon, a clear, friendly font specially designed for children learning to read and write. The labels and sound effects on the pages add fun, engage the reader, and give children the opportunity to distinguish between different levels of communication. Where appropriate, labels, sound effects, or main text may be presented in phonic spelling. Encourage children to imitate the sounds.

As you read the book, you can also take the opportunity to talk about the book itself with appropriate vocabulary, such as "page," "cover," "back," "front," "photograph," "label," and "page number."

You can also extend children's learning by using the books as a springboard for discussion and further activities. There are a few suggestions on the facing page.

22

Pages 4–5: Dinnertime
Encourage children to keep a food diary, either as a group or individually. Divide a big piece of paper into seven sections, one for each day of the week. Encourage children to draw, paint, or stick photos of what they ate for dinner on each day.

Pages 6–7: Getting Ready
Make mini pizzas from homemade salt dough, then bake and paint. Use as a prop in a pretend pizzeria, where children can role play being cooks, serving staff, or customers.

Pages 8–9: Rice
Fill a large box (or sand table) with rice which children can explore and pour using funnels, spoons, scoops, and cups. For multicolored rice, shake up uncooked white rice, food coloring and a little water or white spirit in a sealed plastic bag, then air-dry on a tray for a few hours.

Pages 10–11: Fresh Vegetables
If you have outdoor space, grow vegetables. Peas are rewarding, since most children like to eat them. Otherwise, grow carrot tops. Put each carrot top on wet cotton wool on a saucer and wait for the leaves to sprout. Encourage children to count the fronds or even chart the growth.

Pages 12–13: Pasta and Noodles
Sitting alongside a child at the computer, type "pasta shapes" into an internet search engine. Print off reference of different shapes and their names, which the children can copy to make their own pasta poster.

Pages 14–15: Food from the Sea
Put on some "watery" music, then ask children to dance while role playing different marine animals, such as crab, shark, or octopus.

Pages 16–17: All Kinds of Meat
Create a mural of storefronts. Write the name of each store—for example, butcher, baker, greengrocer, jeweler—and then fill its window with a collage of "produce" (artworks made by the children).

Pages 18–19: Desserts
Find out what children's favorite desserts are, and compile a recipe book illustrated with paintings by the children.

Pages 20–21: Make It: Raita
Make basic raita and then divide it into small portions, each with an additional flavoring such as chopped coriander, raisins, or grated apple. Arrange a blind tasting and see which flavors the children like best.

Index

PARK COUNTY PUBLIC LIBRARY
GUFFEY BRANCH

Picture acknowledgments:
Alamy: 12 (Image State), 15 (Food Folio); **Corbis:** 17 (Hall/Photocuisine);
Evans: 4-5 (Gareth Boden); **Getty:** cover (Foodcollection), 6 (Flynn Larsen),
7 (Stephanie Rausser/Taxi), 8 (Altrendo), 16 (Lee Strickland/Taxi), 19 (Angela
Wyant/Stone); **iStockphoto:** cover tablecloth, 2-3, 22-24 (Gaffera), cover sky,
22-24 (Judy Foldetta), 11 (Bluestocking), 18 (David Hernandez); **Photolibrary:**
9 (Patrick Syder), 10 (Index Stock Imagery), 13 (Foodpix),
20-21 (Andrew Sydenham); **WT-Pix:** 14.